I've Got Jesus...
Now What?

I've Got Jesus...
Now What?

By Carrie Daws

I've Got Jesus...Now What?

© 2017 by Carrie Daws

All rights reserved. Produced in the United States of America. Except as permitted under the United States Copyright Act of 1976, no part of this publication may be reproduced in any form or by any means, or stored in a database or retrieval system, without the prior written permission of the publisher.

ISBN: 978-1-947539-00-6
eISBN: 978-1-947539-01-3

Unless otherwise indicated, Scriptures are taken from THE HOLY BIBLE, NEW INTERNATIONAL VERSION® Copyright © 1973, 1978, 1984, 2011 by Biblica, Inc.™ Used by permission. All rights reserved worldwide.

Cover Design by Jarmal Wilcox
Book layout by Hailey Radabaugh

IMMEASURABLE WORKS
104 Harvest Ln
Raeford, NC 28376, USA
CarrieDaws.com/ImmeasurableWorks

Table of Contents

Spiritual Birth Certificate 9
A Note from the Author 11
What You Need to Know about This Book 13

Part One: Your Beginnings
Chapter One: Salvation 17
    A Summary
    More Detail
Chapter Two: Baptism 29
    A Summary
    More Detail

Part Two: Your Growth Plan
Chapter Three: Daily Time with God 41
    A Summary
    More Detail
Chapter Four: Prayer 51
    A Summary
    More Detail
Chapter Five: Tithing 63
    A Summary
    More Detail
Chapter Six: Fellowship 75
    A Summary
    More Detail

Part Three: Final Thoughts
Chapter Seven: Wrapping It Up 87

Appendix
Recommended Resources 89

My Spiritual Birth Certificate

Name: _____
Date of New Birth: _____
Date Baptized: _____
Person who shared Christ with me: _____
_____

Church: _____
City/State: _____

A Note from the Author

Welcome!

The moment you accepted Jesus as your Savior, you became a member of God's family. The apostle Paul wrote in Ephesians chapter 1 that through our faith in Jesus, we were adopted as sons and daughters. That means you now have a huge family cheering you on, including me!

Perhaps that's a bit overwhelming. Maybe family hasn't been something good in your life, or you fear the expectations other Christians will place upon you.

Take a moment and breathe.

One of the key pieces of information God wants to give you is this: <u>Only His opinion matters</u>. Yes, God will use other people and circumstances to help you along the way, but they should never take precedence over what God says.

That is why hearing God clearly is critical, and that is why I wrote this book.

As you work your way through these pages, I want you to keep two things in mind.

1. First, this is not a race. Getting the information I share is vital, but it's more important that you understand God's heart. The Bible is not a list of rules and regulations. It is a letter from a Father who loves you immensely, who wants to give you wisdom and protect you from harm.
2. And second, Satan, God's enemy—and now yours as well—doesn't want you to get any of this. He doesn't want you to understand how much God loves you. He strives to distract you and will whisper lies to hinder you.

So join me in learning more about what it means to be part of God's family. Don't worry. You don't have to do this perfectly or know the answer to every question. Just take a step forward and turn the page.

We'll get through these first steps together.

Carrie

What You Need to Know about This Book

1. Unless otherwise noted, the Scriptures in this book are from the 2011 edition of the New International Version Bible. You can find free digital copies of this Bible version on the Internet at BibleGateway.com or through the smart phone/tablet app YouVersion.
2. You should invest in a good Bible. What does that mean? Many great Bibles are available, but a *good* Bible is one that you will read and can understand. Check out different translations like the Contemporary English Version or the New Living Translation (also available at BibleGateway.com and on YouVersion).
3. When I list a Bible reference, it will look like this: Psalm 75:1. Psalm is the book of the Bible. The number before the colon (75 in this example) is the chapter of the book, and the number after the colon (1 in this example) is the verse number within that chapter. A couple of special cases:

    a. If you see a number before the book name, it means that more than one book carries that title. For example, 1 Corinthians and 2 Corinthians. If the verse you're reading doesn't make sense, you could be in the wrong book.
    b. Five books of the Bible only have one chapter. This can be written two different ways: Philemon 1:4, or simply Philemon 4. It can be even more confusing when a verse from either the books of 2 John (Second John) or 3 John (Third John) are mentioned.

It will get easier with time, but use your Bible's table of contents to help you as long as you need to.
4. Choose a time and a place where you will most often read your Bible. You can read your Bible anywhere and at any time, but habits start by doing the same thing at the same time in the same place. Designating a room or a chair will encourage you to keep reading your Bible.
5. Finally, it's okay not to answer some questions within these pages. Each question was purposely put on the page to help you think through key concepts, but that doesn't mean you fail Christianity 101 if you skip writing down an answer or two.

With all of that in mind, are you ready to get started? Here we go!

Part One
Your Beginnings

Chapter One: Salvation

A Summary

Every Christian I've ever asked admits to questioning their salvation at some point in their lives. This is a normal—and good—struggle. Some of the greatest men in the Bible struggled with confusion and uncertainty. But it is perseverance in faith that God seeks.

Cementing Our Faith

God gives us assurances to help us cement our faith in Him.

> **Consider John 3:16.**
> *For God so loved the world that He gave His one and only Son, that whoever believes in Him shall not perish but have eternal life.*

> **Consider 1 John 5:11-12.**
> *This is the testimony: God has given us eternal life, and this life is in His Son. Whoever has the Son has life; whoever does not have the Son of God does not have life.*

Believing God's Character

We must also cement our faith in God's character. After all, why should we believe in the promises if we can't trust the promise-giver?

> **Consider 1 Corinthians 1:9**
> *God is faithful, who has called you into fellowship with His Son, Jesus Christ our Lord.*

The book of 1 Corinthians was written by the Apostle Paul who also wrote this:

I have worked much harder, been in prison more frequently, been flogged more severely, and been exposed to death again and again. Five times I received from the Jews the forty lashes minus one. Three times I was beaten with rods, once I was pelted with stones, three times I was shipwrecked, I spent a night and a day in the open sea. 2 Corinthians 11:23-25

All of that turmoil and tragedy, and still Paul was convinced that *God is faithful.*

Consider Isaiah 41:13
For I am the Lord your God who takes hold of your right hand and says to you, Do not fear; I will help you.

God's Seal Upon You

Finally, you can trust your salvation because God gave you the Holy Spirit.

Consider 2 Corinthians 1:21-22
He anointed us, set his seal of ownership on us, and put his Spirit in our hearts as a deposit, guaranteeing what is to come.

Ephesians 1:13-14
And you also were included in Christ when you heard the message of truth, the gospel of your salvation. When you believed, you were marked in him with a seal, the promised Holy Spirit, who is a deposit guaranteeing our inheritance until the redemption of those who are God's possession—to the praise of his glory.

Salvation

More Detail

Every Christian I've ever asked admits to questioning their salvation at some point in their lives. Life gets messy, we fail to do what we know we should, and pretty soon we're wondering if we ever really believed God in the first place. This is a normal—and good—struggle.

One day, you may wonder how to reconcile the Bible with a scientific theory exhorted in the news. Perhaps a dear friend in another religion presents questions you can't answer. Maybe tragedy hits a loved one or you see another massacre reported online, and you wonder how a good God can allow such pain. Or perhaps you grapple with a deep-seated sin that you can't seem to escape from.

Doubt creeps in. Questions arise. And frequently, in these moments of internal battle, God gets very quiet.

Doubt is okay. Some of the greatest men in the Bible struggled with disbelief, apprehension, confusion, suspicion, and uncertainty. Consider these verses from the Psalms:

> *I am weary with my moaning; every night I flood my bed with tears; I drench my couch with my weeping. My eye wastes away because of grief; it grows weak because of all my foes* (Psalm 6:6–7).

> *My God, my God, why have you forsaken me? Why are you so far from saving me, from the words of my groaning? O my God, I cry by day, but you do not answer, and by night, but I find no rest* (Psalm 22:1–2).

O Lord, rebuke me not in your anger, nor discipline me in your wrath! For your arrows have sunk into me, and your hand has come down on me. There is no soundness in my flesh because of your indignation; there is no health in my bones because of my sin. For my iniquities have gone over my head; like a heavy burden, they are too heavy for me (Psalm 38:1–4).

Perhaps one of the greatest stories about this fight with doubt is told in the book of Job. In the first two chapters, readers are given insight to the heavenly wager between God and Satan, yet all Job knows is that in one day he loses his oxen, donkeys, sheep, camels, servants, and children. Shortly thereafter, he is struck *with loathsome sores from the sole of his foot to the crown of his head* (Job 2:7). Now that's a bad week!

But as much as the rest of the book presents Job's cries for answers, it also reveals his faith. In his confusion, he turns to God. In his pain, he knows God holds the solution. No matter what life looked like around him, Job appealed to God, and it was that very perseverance in his faith that mattered. Ultimate steadfastness despite tragedy and uncertainty is what God seeks.

Brothers and sisters, as an example of patience in the face of suffering, take the prophets who spoke in the name of the Lord. As you know, we count as blessed those who have persevered. You have heard of Job's perseverance and have seen what the Lord finally brought about. The Lord is full of compassion and mercy (James 5:10–11).

Cementing Our Faith

So the key to doubt is relying on our faith. And God gives us several assurances to help us cement our faith in Hm.

(Note: If you struggle with the validity of the Bible, check out *The Case for Christ: A Journalist's Personal Investigation of the Evidence for Jesus* by Lee Strobel.)

First, consider John 3:16.
For God so loved the world that He gave His one and only Son, that whoever believes in Him shall not perish but have eternal life.

This is a conditional promise, or a promise of what God will do based on the choice we make. In John chapter 3, the apostle John tells the story of a Pharisee (a Jewish religious man) named Nicodemus who came to Jesus one night to ask Him questions. John 3:16 was part of Jesus's response to him.

In other words, Jesus, God's Son, said *if* we believe in Him, *then* we will have eternal life.

Consider 1 John 5:11–13.
This is the testimony: God has given us eternal life, and this life is in His Son. Whoever has the Son has life; whoever does not have the Son of God does not have life. I write these things to you who believe in the name of the Son of God so that you may know that you have eternal life.

The apostle John wrote these words to the Christians living in Ephesus (modern-day Turkey) somewhere between 60 and 90 A.D. So, John had walked with Jesus on this earth, witnessed His death and resurrection, and lived another thirty to sixty years before writing these words. He experienced persecution under Roman leaders like Herod Agrippa I and learned of the brutal deaths of many Christian friends, including the men closest to Jesus.

And still John wrote, *God has given us eternal life, and this life is in his Son.*

Consider John 5:24
Very truly I tell you, whoever hears My word and believes Him who sent Me has eternal life and will not be judged but has crossed over from death to life.

Again we have John recording what Jesus said. This time, some Jewish leaders were unhappy because Jesus had healed a man on the Sabbath. *In His defense Jesus said to them, "My Father is always at His work to this very day, and I too am working"* (John 5:17). This angered the leaders even more because Jesus *was even calling God His own Father, making Himself equal with God* (John 5:18).

Over the next few verses in John 5, Jesus reveals more about His relationship with God, even delineating some of the responsibilities of God, Jesus, and the Holy Spirit. Then Jesus says the words above, promising eternal life to those who believe God.

BELIEVING GOD'S CHARACTER

The Bible includes a few more instances of similar promises of eternal life, but we must also cement our faith in God's character. After all, why should we believe in the promises if we can't trust the Promise Giver?

Consider 1 Corinthians 1:9
God is faithful, who has called you into fellowship with His Son, Jesus Christ our Lord.

SALVATION

The book of 1 Corinthians was written by the apostle Paul, a zealous Pharisee who actively fought against Christianity (Galatians 1:13–14). The story of how God gained his attention and turned his heart toward Jesus is told in Acts 9:1–30. Before you read those verses, you need to know that Paul also went by the name of Saul.

After spending three years in Arabia and Damascus (Galatians 1:17–18), Paul went to work spreading the gospel of Jesus throughout the Gentile (non-Jew) world. He undertook three major missionary journeys, starting several churches around the Aegean Sea and Asia Minor (modern-day Turkey). The city of Corinth, Greece, hosted one of these churches.

Paul wrote this letter to the Corinthian church about A.D. 55 during his third missionary journey. Second Corinthians was written somewhere between A.D. 55 and 57. In his second letter to Corinth, Paul writes:

I have worked much harder, been in prison more frequently, been flogged more severely, and been exposed to death again and again. Five times I received from the Jews the forty lashes minus one. Three times I was beaten with rods, once I was pelted with stones, three times I was shipwrecked, I spent a night and a day in the open sea, I have been constantly on the move. I have been in danger from rivers, in danger from bandits, in danger from my fellow Jews, in danger from Gentiles; in danger in the city, in danger in the country, in danger at sea; and in danger from false believers. I have labored and toiled and have often gone without sleep; I have known hunger and thirst and have often gone without food; I have been cold and naked. Besides everything else, I face daily the pressure of my concern for all the churches (2 Corinthians 11:23–28).

All of that turmoil and tragedy, and still Paul confidently

wrote *God is faithful.* Was he a fool? Or did he experience more than mere tragedy?

Paul wrote these words to the church in Rome:

For I am convinced that neither death nor life, neither angels nor demons, neither the present nor the future, nor any powers, neither height nor depth, nor anything else in all creation, will be able to separate us from the love of God that is in Christ Jesus our Lord (Romans 8:38–39).

Paul was absolutely convinced that *God is faithful.*

Consider Hebrews 10:23
Let us hold unswervingly to the hope we profess, for he who promised is faithful.

We're not certain who wrote the book of Hebrews, but we do know that it was written to Jewish Christians, probably before the Temple in Jerusalem was destroyed in A.D. 70. Jews didn't approve of the new movement toward Jesus because they didn't recognize Him for who He was. They thought He was a false prophet pulling otherwise devoted Jews away from God. Because of this, Christians faced intense persecution from their own countrymen. The writer of Hebrews encouraged them to remain strong.

Consider Isaiah 41:13
For I am the Lord your God who takes hold of your right hand and says to you, Do not fear; I will help you.

The Bible is full of stories of ordinary people doing amazing things because they allowed God to step into their lives. Abraham, Moses, Ruth, David, Esther, Elijah, and more lived some of Christendom's favorite stories simply because they chose to believe and obey God. He honored their faith, even when they doubted, and incredible—sometimes unbelievable—things happened.

God's faithfulness means you will never walk through any circumstance alone. He will take your right hand and help you.

Consider the Book of Psalms

Psalms is a bit like a collection of personal journals from men like Moses and King David. Within its pages you'll find despair, anger, uncertainty, and joy because the authors recorded their feelings as they faced everyday life.

You will also find a lot of confidence in the Lord.

Psalm 3:3

But you, Lord, are a shield around me, my glory, the One who lifts my head high.

Psalm 20:7

Some trust in chariots and some in horses, but we trust in the name of the Lord our God.

Psalm 37:23–24

The Lord makes firm the steps of the one who delights in him; though he may stumble, he will not fall, for the Lord upholds him with his hand.

Psalm 70:5

I am poor and needy; come quickly to me, O God. You are my help and my deliverer.

God's Seal Upon You

Finally, you can rest assured of your salvation because God placed His seal upon you: the Holy Spirit.

> **Consider 2 Corinthians 1:21–22**
> *He anointed us, set his seal of ownership on us, and put his Spirit in our hearts as a deposit, guaranteeing what is to come.*
>
> **Ephesians 1:13–14**
> *And you also were included in Christ when you heard the message of truth, the gospel of your salvation. When you believed, you were marked in him with a seal, the promised Holy Spirit, who is a deposit guaranteeing our inheritance until the redemption of those who are God's possession—to the praise of his glory.*

The Holy Spirit works within each of us to change us, to help us quit bad habits and form new, good ones. He guides your decisions, encourages you as you read the Bible, and reminds you of the truth you're learning. He is a constant companion and a reminder that God will one day present us with our full inheritance.

Think About It

1. Which of the verses in this chapter means the most to you? Why?

2. What changes have you already seen in your life?

3. How much do you wrestle with doubt? Does this worry you?

A great defense against doubt is to get active in a small group of other Christians. They will stand with you, helping you to learn more about God and His character, cementing your faith, and giving you a safe place to explore uncertainties. Contact your local church office for more information.

Chapter Two: Baptism

A Summary

In many ways, your faith is deeply personal. You must make a decision to believe or not on your own. However, once the decision is made, we cannot keep our choice private.

Personal, But Not Private

Consider Matthew 10:32-33
[Jesus speaking] *Whoever acknowledges me before others, I will also acknowledge before my Father in heaven. But whoever disowns me before others, I will disown before my Father in heaven.*

Consider Matthew 5:14-16
[Jesus speaking] *You are the light of the world. A town built on a hill cannot be hidden. Neither do people light a lamp and put it under a bowl. Instead they put it on its stand, and it gives light to everyone in the house. In the same way, let your light shine before others, that they may see your good deeds and glorify your Father in heaven.*

Baptism is About Obedience

One way to acknowledge God and shine your light is baptism. You've probably seen baptism before, but it isn't as simplistic as submerging yourself in a pool.

Consider Matthew 3:13-16
Jesus left Galilee and went to the Jordan River to be baptized by John. But John kept objecting and said, "I ought

to be baptized by you. Why have you come to me?"

Jesus answered, "For now this is how it should be, because we must do all that God wants us to do." Then John agreed. (Contemporary English Version)

Consider Matthew 28:18-19
Jesus came to them and said, "All authority in heaven and on earth has been given to me. Therefore go and make disciples of all nations, baptizing them in the name of the Father and of the Son and of the Holy Spirit."

The Symbolism Behind Baptism

Many of the words used in the Bible convey a depth of meaning we lose in English because we don't have the picture in our minds that those of Jesus's day did.

First Corinthians 15:3-4 summarizes the gospel message beautifully.
For what I received I passed on to you as of first importance: that Christ died for our sins according to the Scriptures, that he was buried, that he was raised on the third day according to the Scriptures.

And Romans 6:2-4 summarizes what has happened to you.
We are those who have died to sin . . . Or don't you know that all of us who were baptized into Christ Jesus were baptized into his death? We were therefore buried with him through baptism into death in order that, just as Christ was raised from the dead through the glory of the Father, we too may live a new life.

We have died to sin—we don't have to be controlled by it because Jesus gained victory over it. In death, we go down into the grave, i.e., down into the water.

And just as Jesus defeated death and God raised Him from the grave, we too are raised to new life, i.e., brought up out of the water. While we may still live in the same house or go to the same job, we now have the Holy Spirit guiding us and the hope of eternal life in heaven.

Baptism

More Detail

In many ways, your faith is deeply personal. You must think through everything you've heard or read and make a decision to believe or not on your own. Consider Jesus's words in John 14:6, *I am the way and the truth and the life. No one comes to the Father except through me.* In the original language, He used singular pronouns, inferring that each person must choose Jesus for himself. No one can do it for anyone else.

However, once the decision is made, the Bible clearly says that we cannot keep our choice private.

Personal, But Not Private

Consider Matthew 10:32–33
[Jesus speaking] *Whoever acknowledges me before others, I will also acknowledge before my Father in heaven. But whoever disowns me before others, I will disown before my Father in heaven.*

In this chapter of the Bible, the apostle Matthew is telling the story about the time Jesus sent His twelve main disciples out to tell the Jews that "the kingdom of heaven has come near" (Matthew 10:5). Knowing that it can be intimidating to share your beliefs with others, Jesus encouraged them to be bold because God sees them and cares for them. He then uttered the words above, indicating the severe effects of giving in to fear.

Consider Matthew 5:14–16

[Jesus speaking] *You are the light of the world. A town built on a hill cannot be hidden. Neither do people light a lamp and put it under a bowl. Instead they put it on its stand, and it gives light to everyone in the house. In the same way, let your light shine before others, that they may see your good deeds and glorify your Father in heaven.*

These verses are from a section of Scripture dubbed the Sermon on the Mount (Matthew 5–7). One afternoon, Jesus sat down on the side of a mountain and taught all who would stop long enough to listen. Much of it was as counter-cultural to their ears as it is to ours.

These verses indicate to us that we must not remove ourselves from society, no matter how tempting that may be some days. Instead, we should live with integrity and honor, allowing people to watch us as we seek to follow Christ. In doing so, God will receive praise.

Baptism is About Obedience

One way to acknowledge God before others and shine your light to the world around you is baptism. You've probably seen baptism before. In its most basic sense, it is one person, usually a pastor or leader of a church, dunking another person under water. But it isn't really as simplistic as submerging yourself in a pool.

Consider Matthew 3:13–16

Jesus left Galilee and went to the Jordan River to be baptized by John. But John kept objecting and said, "I ought to be baptized by you. Why have you come to me?"

Jesus answered, "For now this is how it should be, because we must do all that God wants us to do." Then John agreed.

So Jesus was baptized. (Contemporary English Version)

This story, also told in Mark 1:9–11 and Luke 3:21–22, shows us John's reaction to Jesus coming to be baptized near the beginning of Jesus's ministry years on the earth. Jesus led by example as often as He could, so His priority on baptism is something we need to pay attention to.

[NOTE: This was Jesus's cousin John who was born to Zechariah and Elizabeth, not the apostle John who wrote four books of the Bible. You can read Cousin John's story in Luke 1 and Luke 3.]

Consider Matthew 28:18–20
Jesus came to them and said, "All authority in heaven and on earth has been given to me. Therefore go and make disciples of all nations, baptizing them in the name of the Father and of the Son and of the Holy Spirit, and teaching them to obey everything I have commanded you. And surely I am with you always, to the very end of the age."

These were some of the last instructions Jesus gave to His disciples after rising from the dead and before returning to heaven. He told them that two of their primary duties were to baptize and teach.

Consider Acts 2:36–38
"Therefore let all Israel be assured of this: God has made this Jesus, whom you crucified, both Lord and Messiah."

When the people heard this, they were cut to the heart and said to Peter and the other apostles, "Brothers, what shall we do?"

BAPTISM

Peter replied, "Repent and be baptized, every one of you, in the name of Jesus Christ for the forgiveness of your sins. And you will receive the gift of the Holy Spirit."

Jesus returns to heaven, leaving His disciples with one final instruction: *"Do not leave Jerusalem, but wait for the gift my Father promised"* (Acts 1:4). This gift was the Holy Spirit, given to them on the Jewish holiday Shavuot, or Feast of Weeks, which celebrated Moses receiving the law from God on Mount Sinai (that story is told beginning in Exodus 19). The Christian celebration of the Holy Spirit coming to God's people is called Pentecost.

When the Holy Spirit came, the disciples began to speak in other languages—languages they didn't know! It created quite a commotion, and a crowd gathered. Pretty soon, Peter stood and told everyone about Jesus. Some scoffed and walked away, but many wanted to know more, and Peter kept his words faithful to the instructions he'd received from Jesus: Repent and be baptized.

Another example of a disciple following through on Jesus's command to baptize believers is found in Acts 8:26–39.

Consider 1 John 2:3–6
We know that we have come to know him if we keep his commands. Whoever says, "I know him," but does not do what he commands is a liar, and the truth is not in that person. But if anyone obeys his word, love for God is truly made complete in them. This is how we know we are in him: Whoever claims to live in him must live as Jesus did.

The apostle John wrote these words somewhere around A.D. 85-90. He'd lived a long life and seen many things—blessings and persecutions. Yet he was still utterly convinced that those who love God must follow Jesus's commands and His example.

> **Consider John 14:15, 21**
> [Jesus speaking] *If you love me, keep my commands . . . Whoever has my commands and keeps them is the one who loves me. The one who loves me will be loved by my Father, and I too will love them and show myself to them.*

These words, spoken by Jesus and recorded by the apostle John, relate to us how important obeying God is. Each act of obedience carries the message of love within it. And those who love Jesus will be loved by God.

The Symbolism Behind Baptism

Many of the words and phrases used in the Bible convey a depth of meaning we often lose in our English translation because we don't have the picture in our minds that the Jews of Jesus's day did. So I want to take a moment to give you this perspective on baptism.

> **First Corinthians 15:3–4 summarizes the gospel message beautifully.**
> *For what I received I passed on to you as of first importance: that Christ died for our sins according to the Scriptures, that he was buried, that he was raised on the third day according to the Scriptures.*

> **And Romans 6:1–4 summarizes what has happened to you.**
> *Shall we go on sinning so that grace may increase? By no means! We are those who have died to sin; how can we live in it any longer? Or don't you know that all of us who were*

baptized into Christ Jesus were baptized into his death? We were therefore buried with him through baptism into death in order that, just as Christ was raised from the dead through the glory of the Father, we too may live a new life.

In the minds of first century Christians, the two were inseparably linked. We have died to sin—not that we won't sin any more. We just don't have to be controlled by it because, through Jesus's death and resurrection, He gained victory over it. In death, we go down into the grave, i.e., down into the water.

And just as Jesus defeated death and God raised Him from the grave, we too are raised to new life, i.e., brought up out of the water. While we may still live in the same house or go to the same job, we now have the Holy Spirit guiding us, our Christian family cheering us on, and the grand hope of eternal life in heaven.

Baptism is an act of obedience that exquisitely demonstrates our internal reality. Our old life is gone; our new life waits.

Think About It

1. Which of the verses in this chapter means the most to you? Why?

2. If you have not yet been baptized, is something holding you back?

3. Does this first section on salvation and baptism bring any questions to your mind?

Fears, doubts, and questions are three of the reasons we need other Christians around us. If you have joined a Bible study or small group, take your concerns and questions to them and let them share their stories and wisdom with you.

If you have not yet plugged into a Bible study or small group, why not? What is keeping you from doing so? What can you do to overcome your obstacles?

Part Two
Your Growth Plan

One of the things God wants is for you to become a mature follower of Christ. The apostle Paul talks about this in Ephesians 4:11–15.

> *Christ chose some of us to be apostles, prophets, missionaries, pastors, and teachers, so that his people would learn to serve and his body would grow strong. This will continue until we are united by our faith and by our understanding of the Son of God. Then we will be mature, just as Christ is, and we will be completely like him.*

> *We must stop acting like children. We must not let deceitful people trick us by their false teachings, which are like winds that toss us around from place to place. Love should always make us tell the truth. Then we will grow in every way and be more like Christ, the head* (Contemporary English Version).

It's one thing to tell someone to grow up; it's another thing for us to know how to do it and make the choice to follow through. As children, our bodies grew into adulthood without much effort on our part, but we each had to put some work in so that we also grew mentally and emotionally. Likewise, spiritual maturity requires a bit of effort in four key areas: daily time with God, prayer, tithing, and fellowship.

Chapter Three: Daily Time with God

A Summary

You can find thousands of blog posts and hundreds of books offering advice for your time with God, but it should be as individual as you are.

Why *Daily* Time?

Life is busy. Our calendars already overflow with appointments and obligations, and now you have one more thing to make room for in your schedule. But think about the communication that needs to happen for a relationship to grow.

Remember this: When God thinks about you, He craves an intimate, personal relationship. And that only happens with regular, daily time.

> **Consider Psalm 5:3**
> *In the morning, Lord, you hear my voice; in the morning I lay my requests before you and wait expectantly.*

Many of the psalms pour out praise about God, and many others reveal deep pain or direct anger to God. The authors shared all their emotions with God whenever they were feeling them.

Quantity? Or Quality?

Books, websites that will email you daily devotions, and smart phone app stores with digital options perfect for morning commutes or frequent travelers. What should you read during your time with God? Whatever is appropriate for your season of life and whatever God is asking you to read.

Consider King Saul

The first king of Israel was Saul, and during his reign, the Philistine army loomed large in the area. First Samuel 13:5 says, *The Philistines assembled to fight Israel, with . . . soldiers as numerous as the sand on the seashore.* And they possessed weapons Israel could only dream of.

The Israelites were afraid. Saul knew He needed God's blessing if Israel was going to win. So he called for the prophet Samuel, who said he would come. Saul waited until he grew impatient. He offered the sacrifices to God, hoping for God's blessing. Instead, he was confronted with his disobedience.

> *"You have done a foolish thing," Samuel said. "You have not kept the command the Lord your God gave you"* (1 Samuel 13:13).

More than our sacrifice of time or energy or money, God wants our obedience. What you are reading matters less than the discipline of daily reading. And above all, focus on reading what God wants you to read.

Daily Time with God

More Detail

Growing up, I came across a lot of different plans for what is sometimes called *Quiet Time*, which is time I spend focused on God each day. Well-meaning Christians spouted formulas for the perfect way to make the most out of those moments. Today, you can find thousands of blog posts and hundreds of books offering each writer's best advice and devotional thoughts.

Can I tell you something? My quiet time looks very different from my young adult daughter's quiet time. And from my friend's quiet time. And from my mother's quiet time. And it should look different.

While I'll give you some tips and hints, I want you to under-stand one vital key to your time with God: it should be as individual as you are. God made us unique. He filled us with different passions to thrive in, and He blessed us with diverse activities that appeal to us. Don't let someone's formula for the perfect quiet time lock you in a routine that doesn't fit you or your life well.

Cement that into your thinking; settle it deep in your heart.

Why Daily Time?

Is it really necessary to spend time every single day with God? I understand the question. Life is busy. Our calendars already overflow with appointments and obligations, and now you have one more thing to make room for in your schedule.

But think about it this way: How much communication needs to happen for a relationship to grow? Remember when you first met your best friend or spouse? And when you figured out how important they were to your life, how did that change your mindset? Was it easier or harder to make room for them among your other responsibilities?

When God thinks about you, He craves an intimate, personal relationship—one that involves you getting to know each other far better than you know your spouse or best friend. And that kind of closeness only happens with regular, daily time.

In the Bible, the prophet Samuel declared that God sought a man after His heart to be Israel's king (1 Samuel 13:14). This man turned out to be David, the youngest son of Jesse and a humble shepherd who would soon kill the mighty giant Goliath (1 Samuel 17). Since God gave David that title, we should consider David's habits about spending time with God so we better understand what a person after God's heart does.

In Psalm 5:3, David says he lays out his requests before God and waits in expectation in the morning. In Psalm 6:6, David mentions crying out to God all night. Many of the psalms pour out praise about God, and many others reveal deep pain or direct anger to God. I imagine David shaking his head in wonder at the stupidity of man when I read Psalm 2, and he begs for mercy in Psalm 39. David shared all his emotions with God whenever he was feeling them.

If we turn our focus a little deeper, though, we can find two important insights in David's relationship with God. First, Psalm 16:8 says, *I keep my eyes always on the Lord.* David not only spent regular time with God, he set his focus on God. He strived to live his life in God's perspective, drawing upon God's wisdom and strength.

But let's not ignore Psalm 17:6, which says, *I call on You, my God, for You will answer me.* More than merely seeking God, David expected God to answer when David called out to Him. More often than I'd like to admit, I seek God's answer but never hang around long enough to hear it.

Don't miss either one of these critical attributes in your own relationship with God.

QUANTITY? OR QUALITY?

Bookstores carry a plethora of books to help you focus your time with God. The Internet contains hundreds of websites that will email you daily devotions, and smart phone app stores provide digital options perfect for morning commutes or frequent travelers. Some churches have even jumped on board, publishing Bible reading plans so the whole congregation is on the same page.

These are all great options, and I have utilized each one at different times in my life. But you need to make sure that what you are reading during your devotion time is appropriate for your season of life and what God is asking you to do.

Maybe He's asking you to read the entire Bible through in a year. That's an incredible journey, and I highly recommend everyone do that—but this may not be the year God wants you to tackle that kind of reading.

Maybe He's asking you to read through a book on prayer, but it seems like everyone you know is doing the church reading plan. It's okay to read the book on prayer. In fact, it's better if that's what God asked you to do.

The first king of Israel was Saul, a man the Bible describes *as handsome a young man as could be found anywhere in Israel, and he was a head taller than anyone else.* He was the son of a man of standing—an important and respected man in Israel.

During Saul's reign, the Philistine army loomed large in the area. First Samuel 13:5 says, *The Philistines assembled to fight Israel, with three thousand chariots, six thousand charioteers, and soldiers as numerous as the sand on the seashore.* They possessed weapons Israel could only dream of. In fact, at this time in their history, Israel didn't have iron weapons. *On the day of battle not a soldier with Saul and Jonathan had a sword or spear in his hand; only Saul and his son Jonathan had them* (1 Samuel 13:22).

The Israelites were afraid. The Bible says, *When the Israelites saw that their situation was critical and that their army was hard pressed, they hid in caves and thickets, among the rocks, and in pits and cisterns. Some Hebrews* [another name for the Israelites] *even crossed the Jordan to the land of Gad and Gilead. Saul remained at Gilgal, and all the troops with him were quaking with fear.*

Saul knew He needed God's blessing if Israel was going to win. So he called for the prophet Samuel, who said he would arrive in seven days. Saul waited, and more men abandoned him. Finally, on the seventh day, Saul wouldn't wait any more. He offered the sacrifices to God, hoping for God's blessing. Instead, he was confronted with his disobedience.

> *Just as he finished making the offering, Samuel arrived, and Saul went out to greet him.*
>
> *"What have you done?" asked Samuel.*
>
> *Saul replied, "When I saw that the men were scattering, and that you did not come at the set time, and that the Philistines were assembling at Mikmash, I thought, 'Now the Philistines will come down against me at Gilgal, and I have not sought the Lord's favor.' So I felt compelled to offer the burnt offering."*
>
> *"You have done a foolish thing," Samuel said. "You have not kept the command the Lord your God gave you; if you had, he would have established your kingdom over Israel for all time. But now your kingdom will not endure; the Lord*

has sought out a man after his own heart and appointed him ruler of his people, because you have not kept the Lord's command" (1 Samuel 13:10–14).

More than our sacrifice of time or energy or money, God wants our obedience. Some years I've read through the entire Bible, and some years I've read through just the New Testament. Some years I've read through yearly devotionals, and some years I've just focused on reading something—even if it was only a verse or two—every single day.

What you are reading matters less than the discipline of daily reading. And above all, focus on reading what God wants you to read.

How Do I Know What God Wants Me to Read?

That is a big question. We all want to be certain that we are following God's plan, but in my life it's often seemed like His thoughts were ambiguous at best. I've wrestled with questions like:

- Should I read the devotional that appeals to me, or stick with just reading through a book of the Bible? Or should I read a little of each every day—more is better, right?
- Do regular, nonfiction books that help me be a better Christian count? Or only books set up like devotions? Or only the Bible?
- Should I read straight through the Bible? Or the New Testament? Or can I hop around to different books or stories? Can I just read about Abraham or Moses or David?
- If I follow a reading plan, which one should I choose? Is one plan (or author) better than another?

Let me encourage you with this good news: When it comes to reading the Bible, you really can't mess this up. God is in all of it, and He can speak to you through any of it.

That said, though, a plan is a good idea. No one meanders their way into an intimate relationship, and remember, that's what God wants. In her book, *Discerning the Voice of God: How to Recognize When God is Speaking*, Priscilla Shirer wrote, "The more acquainted you become with the Word, the more accurately you'll be able to hear from Him. The Bible provides the framework into which His messages to you will come" (page 128).

If you want to know when God is speaking to you in other areas of your life—from major decisions to minor concerns—you need to spend regular time in the Bible. You need to read big portions and study small passages. You need to consume books by authors who can explain the Jewish mindset, ancient history, and foreign cultures. And you need to ask God to help you understand and remember it.

That means that everything I've mentioned so far and more has a place in your daily time with God. Regular nonfiction books and devotionals. Bible reading plans and character studies. Reading straight through either or both of the Testaments and skipping around to your favorite stories.

Feel free to add music if that speaks to your soul. Or drawing. Or journaling. Take your Bible outside to watch the sunrise. Listen to an audio Bible while you jog around your neighborhood. Use the passions and talents God put into you as you open His Word and spend time with Him.

Think About It

1. Which part of this chapter means the most to you? Why?

2. Do you think developing the habit of reading the Bible daily will be easy or difficult for you? What is one thing you can do to make it easier?

3. Do you still have any doubts or hesitations about adding this habit to your daily routine? Take these concerns and questions to your small group and let them share their stories and wisdom with you.

If you have not yet plugged into a Bible study or small group, why not? Do you not see the value in them, or is your life too busy for another meeting in your week? Try thinking outside the box: Could you meet another Christian for a morning run, or meet twice a month for lunch?

Chapter Four: Prayer

A Summary

A model prayer from Jesus is found in Luke 11:2–4 and Matthew 6: 9–13.

Consider Matthew 6:9–13
Our Father in heaven, hallowed be Your name, Your kingdom come, Your will be done, on earth as it is in heaven. Give us today our daily bread. And forgive us our debts, as we also have forgiven our debtors. And lead us not into temptation, but deliver us from the evil one.

Everything in the first half of the Lord's Prayer focuses on God. The second half of the Lord's Prayer turns the attention on us.

Is That All We Need to Know?

God gives us many examples throughout the pages of Scripture, and both Jesus and the apostles add tips and good advice.

Consider Luke 11:11–13
Which of you fathers, if your son asks for a fish, will give him a snake instead? Or if he asks for an egg, will give him a scorpion? If you then, though you are evil, know how to give good gifts to your children, how much more will your Father in heaven give the Holy Spirit to those who ask him!

In Luke 18:1–8, Jesus tells a story to show us that we shouldn't give up praying when it seems as if God doesn't hear us. In 1 Thessalonians 5:17, the apostle Paul admonishes us to continually choose an attitude of prayer, and in 1 John 1:8–9, John reminds us to confess our sins so that God will forgive us *and purify us from all unrighteousness.*

Perhaps one of the best books to teach us about prayer is Psalms. The authors poured out the emotion they were feeling at the time, baring their hearts in all kinds of circumstances. They held nothing back from God, but shared their anger, confusion, turmoil, sorrow, and praise with Him. Many Christians turn to this book when they are unsure how to communicate what they are feeling.

Some Big Words

Much like doctors use medical jargon without trying, Christians who've attended church for years tend to use some big words when they talk about prayer.

Adoration. Offering praise to God. Psalm 150 is a good example.

Confession. Admission. While a Christian is granted eternal life by accepting Jesus as Savior, our relationship with God is hindered when we refuse to confess the sin in our life.

Supplication. Humble prayer. It is asking God for those things that are on your mind.

Petition. Broadly defined, this making a request. Sometimes churches use it more narrowly to mean requests you make for your personal benefit.

Intercession. Prayer on another's behalf.

Prayer

More Detail

A quick search in the Amazon Kindle store revealed more than 28,000 books on prayer. That's a lot of words on a topic of immense importance to Christianity. And yet with all the help available to us, many Christians fear praying out loud in front of other people or struggle to maintain vital prayer lives. Is it really that complicated?

Most of us have heard or read beautiful prayers. Some people have a natural rhythm that puts spoken words together well. Prayers flow out of them, seemingly without effort. I do not possess this ability. My prayers stumble about, usually hitting the high points, but frequently wandering from one topic to another as thoughts rush to mind. Often I don't know what to ask for, so I trust God to understand my meandering and offer me what is best in return.

The good news is that my humble rambling is wholly acceptable to God.

Remember what I said before about God's desire? Ultimately, He wants an intimate relationship with us, and the best way for that to happen is through communication. Getting to know God by reading the Bible is important because that teaches us more about Him. But He will also speak to us in quiet whispers, and He wants to hear from us too. Good relationships include both people talking and listening to each other. In other words, we can't just read our Bible, list our concerns for the day, and expect God to move. We must talk to God, and we must listen for God to speak to us.

That's the essence of prayer: talking to God and listening for His response. And however you best do that—whether the words flow smoothly or you traipse around like me—it's acceptable to God.

How Do I Pray?

It seems like an innocent question, but a lot of fear and uncertainty lies within it.

- Some people want to get it right, as in use the perfect formula or process. While many have written easy-to-remember tips and acrostics, you don't have to use one to get God's attention.
- Some people want to know the proper topics with which they should approach the Creator of the universe. Much like a good, earthly daddy, God wants to know everything about you, even if it doesn't seem important in the grand scale of the universe.
- Some want the reassurance that grammar and fancy words really aren't necessary. They aren't. God wants to hear from you, no matter whether you speak in country slang or highly proper English.

Does it relieve a little stress if I tell you that the disciples once asked Jesus about prayer? Luke 11:1 says, *One day Jesus was praying in a certain place. When he finished, one of his disciples said to him, "Lord, teach us to pray, just as John taught his disciples."*

John, Jesus's cousin, was the man God sent to prepare the crowds to hear the message Jesus would speak. Prior to Jesus starting His ministry, John preached to many, gathering a following, teaching them much like Jesus would one day do. You can read more about this in Luke chapters 1 and 3.

The disciple's statement to Jesus in Luke 11 indicates that John taught his followers a specific, distinctive prayer that identified them as part of the group. Jesus's followers wanted a unique prayer of their own, and Jesus conceded in verses 2–4. It is commonly called the Lord's Prayer or the Disciple's Prayer.

A longer version of the prayer is found in Jesus's Sermon on the Mount, suggesting that Jesus repeated the prayer to His followers. Clearly, the disciples adopted it, as evidenced by the early church having new members say it immediately after baptism and during their first communion.

The prayer goes like this:

Our Father in heaven,
hallowed be Your name,
Your kingdom come,
Your will be done,
on earth as it is in heaven.
Give us today our daily bread.
And forgive us our debts,
as we also have forgiven our debtors.
And lead us not into temptation,
but deliver us from the evil one (Matthew 6:9–13).

While this is a great prayer, you need to understand that Jesus wasn't dictating this as the only way to pray. He shared a format and entrusted us with principles. He wanted us to grasp the attitude of the prayer more than the words themselves.

Focusing on God

Everything in the first half of the Lord's Prayer focuses on God. Jesus begins by teaching His disciples to start with worship. This is an important principle, and one easy to forget or underutilize.

In his book *The Necessity of Prayer*, E.M. Bounds writes, "The faith which creates powerful praying is the faith which centers itself on a powerful person. Faith in Christ's ability to *do* and to do *greatly*, is the faith which prays greatly" (The Complete Works of E.M. Bounds on Prayer, page 14). If you want to ask God for incredible things and see Him respond in miraculous ways, you must start by centering yourself on God.

In the Lord's Prayer, the word *Father* indicates a familiarity with God that was unheard of in Jesus's day, particularly among the Jews. However, the intimacy was balanced with the reminder of God's holiness and sovereignty with the phrase *hallowed be Your name*. The word *name* also carries with it a sense of God's character. To refer or say God's name was to include all that He is, e.g., supreme, holy, faithful, provider, healer, creator, etc.

Your kingdom come, Your will be done, on earth as it is in heaven. These three phrases again acknowledge God's sovereignty. In saying this, we acknowledge trust that His plans on this earth will be accomplished just as surely as His plans in heaven will be.

Focusing on Us

The second half of the Lord's Prayer turns the attention on us. It seems to start simply by asking for God to *give us today our daily bread.* The words Luke used make it clear that this is a continual request. We trust God has provided all of our needs for today, so we ask that He similarly provide all our needs for tomorrow.

When Jesus said, "*Forgive us our debts,*" every Jewish mind in his audience understood Him to be talking about their sin. He inferred regular confession of sins, and this understanding is echoed by the apostle John in 1 John 1:9. *If we confess our sins, he is faithful and just and will forgive us our sins and purify us from all unrighteousness.* Jesus knew that sin that is ignored causes problems in relationships—both between people on the earth and between a person and God.

The next line is one of the more unpopular phrases of the Bible. Jesus attached a condition for God forgiving our sins: *as we also have forgiven our debtors.* Now understand that this isn't a condition of salvation. Remember, Jesus was teaching attitudes and principles. He wanted us to know that following Him meant doing things differently. It means checking our heart attitudes, not merely following a prescribed set of rules perfectly. As the New American Commentary on Luke states, "The hand that reaches out to God for forgiveness cannot withhold forgiveness to others."[1]

Perhaps you have been deeply hurt. Maybe someone invaded your world so severely that you can't even stand the thought of them. I understand that kind of anger and pain as I too experienced something tragic in my childhood. Can I tell you that it's a heavy burden, and God doesn't want you to carry it? Please understand that I'm not insisting you forgive and forget; that's unreasonable and minimizes what you've endured. Instead, tell God about the pain and your feelings about the other person. Allow Him to love you, even in this dark place.

The next phrase Jesus says can also be confusing: *And lead us not into temptation.* Would God lead us into temptation? If He did, would He leave us there on our own? First, let's take the counsel of Jesus's half-brother James, one of the leaders of the church in Jerusalem. He wrote, *When tempted, no one should say, "God is tempting me." For God cannot be tempted by evil, nor does he tempt anyone* (James 1:13). Additionally, we know that when we are tempted, God will not abandon us. The apostle Paul wrote in 1 Corinthians 10:13, *God is faithful; he will not let you be tempted beyond what you can bear. But when you are tempted, he will also provide a way out so that you can endure it.*

So what did Jesus mean? I think His words in Mark 14 give us an important clue. In the final hours before Jesus's arrest, trial, and crucifixion, He went to the Garden of Gethsemane to pray. *Jesus said to His disciples, "Sit here while I pray." He took Peter, James and John along with Him, and He began to be deeply distressed and troubled. "My soul is overwhelmed with sorrow to the point of death," He said to them. "Stay here and keep watch"* (Mark 14:32–24).

After praying for a while, *He returned to His disciples and found them sleeping. "Simon," He said to Peter, "are you asleep? Couldn't you keep watch for one hour? Watch and pray so that you will not fall into temptation. The spirit is willing, but the flesh is weak"* (Mark 14:37–38).

Much like those disciples so long ago, our spirits are willing to do all that God asks of us, but our flesh—the human side of us that seeks to fill our selfish desires—is weak. Knowing this about us, I believe Jesus wanted us to understand that it was appropriate to ask God for the courage and tenacity to stand strong in the face of temptation. It's good to know our weak-nesses and to ask our Heavenly Father to provide the support and reinforcement we need.

Finally, Jesus ends the prayer with the request for God to *deliver us from the evil one.* That may seem like common sense, but its wisdom is easy to discount or forget.

Is That All We Need to Know?

Thankfully, the Bible is full of information about prayer. God gives us many examples throughout the pages of Scripture, and both Jesus and the apostles add tips and good advice. For example, Jesus encourages us to approach God with our requests. He says, *Which of you fathers, if your son asks for a fish, will give him a snake instead? Or if he asks for an egg, will give him a scorpion? If you then, though you are evil, know how to give good gifts to your children, how much more will your Father in heaven give the Holy Spirit to those who ask him* (Luke 11:11–13)!

In Luke 18:1–8, Jesus tells a story to show us that we shouldn't give up praying when it seems as if God doesn't hear us. In 1 Thessalonians 5:17, the apostle Paul admonishes us to continually choose an attitude of prayer, and in 1 John 1:8–9, John reminds us to confess our sins so that God will forgive us *and purify us from all unrighteousness.*

Perhaps one of the best books to teach us about prayer is Psalms. The authors poured out the emotion they were feeling at the time, baring their hearts in all kinds of circumstances. They held nothing back from God, but shared their anger, confusion, turmoil, sorrow, and praise with Him. Many Christians turn to this book when they are unsure how to communicate what they are feeling.

Some Big Words

Much like doctors use medical jargon without trying, Christians who've attended church for years tend to use some big words when they talk about prayer. Let's discuss a few of those terms so you won't be caught unaware when you hear them.

Adoration. Dictionary.com defines adoration as "the act of paying honor, as to a divine being; worship."[2] In other words, adoration is simply offering praise to God. Psalm 150 is a good example.

Confession. You are probably familiar with this word, but the dictionary says it is "acknowledgement; avowal; admission."[3] While a Christian is granted eternal life by accepting Jesus as Savior, our relationship with God is hindered when we refuse to confess the sin in our life. Psalm 66:17–18 says, *I cried out to Him with my mouth; His praise was on my tongue. If I had cherished sin in my heart, the Lord would not have listened.*

Supplication. Dictionary.com defines this as "humble prayer, entreaty, or petition."[4] It is asking God for those things that are on your mind and in your heart.

Petition. Broadly defined, the dictionary says this is "a request made for something desired, especially a respectful or humble request, as to a superior or to one of those in authority."[5] Sometimes, in the church world, this word is used more narrowly to mean requests you make of God for your personal benefit.

Intercession. This is "a prayer to God on behalf of another."[6] Any time you spend asking God to meet the needs of someone besides yourself, you intercede for that person.

Think About It

1. Which part of this chapter means the most to you? Why?

2. First Thessalonians 5:16–18 says, *Rejoice always, pray continually, give thanks in all circumstances; for this is God's will for you in Christ Jesus.* Which one of those three will be the easiest for you? Which will be most difficult, and what can you do to encourage yourself to improve on it?

3. What comes to mind when you think about sharing everything you think and feel with God? Does being open about emotions come naturally to you, or do you tend to hold things back? Talk to God about this, and ask Him to help you be more open with Him.

---

[1] R. H. Stein, *Luke*, vol. 24 (Nashville, TN: Broadman & Holman Publishers, 1992), 326.
[2] "Adoration." *Dictionary.com*. Dictionary.com, n.d. Web. 25 Apr. 2017.
[3] "Confession." *Dictionary.com*. Dictionary.com, n.d. Web. 25 Apr. 2017.
[4] "Supplication." *Dictionary.com*. Dictionary.com, n.d. Web. 25 Apr. 2017.
[5] "Petition." *Dictionary.com*. Dictionary.com, n.d. Web. 25 Apr. 2017.
[6] "Intercession." *Dictionary.com*. Dictionary.com, n.d. Web. 25 Apr. 2017.

Chapter Five: Tithing

A Summary

Our word *tithe*, which literally means *one tenth*, originates in Old English, although its practice is ancient and widespread. Stories of old tell of disparate peoples offering a tenth of their money, produce, or labor for various religious activities, from places as diverse as Athens, Rome, Egypt, and China.

The first recorded tithe in the Bible is in a story about Abram and his nephew Lot in Genesis 14. A great war broke out be-tween nine kings, four against five. The kings of the lands where Lot lived fled, and the opposing kings seized goods, food, and people, including Lot. One man escaped and reported this to Abram (Genesis 14:13), and Abram called his fighting men. Genesis 14:16 says, *He recovered all the goods and brought back his relative Lot and his possessions, together with the women and the other people.*

When Abram returned, one of the kings who had run brought out bread and wine (Genesis 14:18). The author of Genesis writes that this king *was priest of God Most High, and he blessed Abram, saying, "Blessed be Abram by God Most High, Creator of heaven and earth. And praise be to God Most High, who delivered your enemies into your hand"* (verses 18–20). At this point, the Bible records that Abram gave the king *a tenth of everything* (verse 20).

Abram doesn't give a tithe to the priest in order to gain a blessing or God's favor. He'd already won the battle. Instead, Abram offered the tithe in acknowledgement of God's blessing and favor.

The True Purpose of the Tithe

The law recorded in Leviticus, Numbers, and Deuteronomy

includes many instructions for tithing. The Israelites were reminded that the tithe *belongs to the Lord; it is holy to the Lord* (Leviticus 27:30). In returning a portion to God, all the Jews recognized God's provision for today and their dependence upon Him for tomorrow.

In addition to supporting the priests and the Tabernacle, the tithe was used to support community festivals, orphans, widows, and travelers (Deuteronomy 12:5–7; 14:22–23, 27–29). And God was serious about His people understanding that the tithe was a big deal.

Consider Malachi 3:8–10.
"Will a mere mortal rob God? Yet you rob Me.

"But you ask, 'How are we robbing You?'

"In tithes and offerings. You are under a curse—your whole nation—because you are robbing Me. Bring the whole tithe into the storehouse, that there may be food in My house. Test Me in this," says the Lord Almighty, "and see if I will not throw open the floodgates of heaven and pour out so much blessing that there will not be room enough to store it."

Tithing is about understanding that God is sovereign. He has supreme power and authority, which means He owns everything and can do with it what He chooses (Psalm 24:1, 115:3). In His wisdom, He elects to allow us a portion to use as we see fit. By giving back to Him a small percentage, we acknowledge His rule and show appreciation for all He's given us. It's a response of love—just like it was for both Abram and Jacob.

Tithing

More Detail

Do you want to skip this chapter? It's okay to be honest. Many of us get very uncomfortable when money comes up for discussion, particularly if we think we're going to be guilted into giving some away when we don't really want to.

The truth is that our feelings about money reveals what is in our hearts: both ours and those around us. And often we don't like what we see. Consider the recent controversy about wages for workers in fast food restaurants. Many who want to dramatically increase the pay boldly declare that a worker is worth his pay . . . at least until they go to buy something themselves. Then they want to know why the cost of [insert one of the desires of your heart here] is so high.

It may surprise some that the concept *a worker is worth his wage* is straight from the mouth of Jesus. Matthew and Luke both tell stories of when Jesus sent out disciples and uttered these words:

> *Jesus called his twelve disciples to him and gave them authority to drive out impure spirits and to heal every disease and sickness . . . "As you go, proclaim this message: 'The kingdom of heaven has come near.' Heal the sick, raise the dead, cleanse those who have leprosy, drive out demons. Freely you have received; freely give. Do not get any gold or silver or copper to take with you in your belts—no bag for the journey or extra shirt or sandals or a staff, for the worker is worth his keep"* (Matthew 10:1, 7–10).

> *The Lord appointed seventy-two others and sent them two by two ahead of him to every town and place where he was about to go. He told them, ". . . Go! I am sending you out like lambs among wolves. Do not take a purse or bag or sandals; and do not greet anyone on the road. When you enter a house, first say, 'Peace to this house.' If someone who promotes peace is there, your peace will rest on them; if not, it will return to you. Stay there, eating and drinking whatever they give you, for the worker deserves his wages. Do not move around from house to house* (Luke 10:1–7).

Similar stories. Similar instructions. In both cases, the worker worth his keep was someone sent by God to proclaim the good news about Jesus. Does this mean that only pastors and missionaries are worth their keep? Of course not. But we should note that the provision expected was for necessities: shelter and food, possibly clean clothes. And, once someone accepted the disciple into his home, he was not to go looking for better accommodations—in Luke, Jesus even addresses this temptation when He says, "Do not move around from house to house."

In our modern American society, most of us have considerably more than we need. From overflowing closets to chilled or heated homes to time for copious amounts of television, movies, and social media, we all tend to be hoarders of God's blessings. This isn't necessarily bad. God wants to bless us and wants us to enjoy His blessings.

But the selfishness inherent in our hearts is revealed when entitlement sneaks out of our mouths. Maybe you've said or thought these things like I have:

- I work hard, so I deserve [*insert your favorite indulgence or pastime here*].

- I already give more [*money, time, effort, etc.*] than [*insert the name of the person or organization that you think doesn't give or do enough here*].
- I can't give [*money, time, effort, etc.*] right now because I'm already facing [*insert whatever difficulty comes to mind*].

The marketing all around us reinforces many of these ideas. Who comes to mind with phrases like *You're worth it* or *Have it your way* or *Giving 110%*? What about that empathetic friend who says, *You already do so much* or *You have so much on your plate right now.*

Before we go any further, let me tell you that you are precious and loved by the Lord (Isaiah 43:4, Matthew 10:29–31). I also want to reinforce the idea that God doesn't expect you to do it all, and a healthy balance between work, family, and ministry is important.

But let us also remember what drove us to God in the first place: our sin. What we *deserve* is condemnation and death (Romans 3:23, 6:23). God, in His great love for us, provided Jesus on the cross to gift us with eternal life (John 3:16). Everything in our lives apart from eternal punishment is a blessing.

With that in mind, the starting place for tithing is the same starting place for everything else in our lives: God. You should always be asking, *What does God want me to do?* Does God want you to tithe? And if so, what does that look like? These are the questions we'll focus on next.

The Early History of the Tithe

Our word *tithe*, which literally means *one tenth*, originates in Old English, although its practice is ancient and widespread. Stories of old tell of disparate peoples offering a tenth of their money, produce, or labor for various religious activities, from places as diverse as Athens, Rome, Egypt, and China.

The first recorded tithe in the Bible is in Genesis 14. God spoke to a man named Abram (later renamed Abraham), telling him, *Go from your country, your people and your father's household to the land I will show you. I will make you into a great nation, and I will bless you; I will make your name great, and you will be a blessing* (Genesis 12:1–2). Pretty impressive promise, right? Abram follows God, and his nephew Lot goes with him.

It wasn't long before the two men realized *the land could not support them while they stayed together, for their possessions were so great that they were not able to stay together* (Genesis 13:6). So they split up, Lot going to the plain of Jordan south of the Dead Sea while Abram went to the land of Canaan, roughly located in modern-day Lebanon, Syria, Jordan, and Israel.

A great war broke out in Lot's area between nine kings, four against five. The kings of the lands where Lot lived fled, and the opposing kings seized goods, food, and people, including Lot. One man escaped and reported this to Abram (Genesis 14:13), and Abram called his fighting men to him. Genesis 14:16 says, *He recovered all the goods and brought back his relative Lot and his possessions, together with the women and the other people.*

When Abram returned, one of the kings who had run—the King of Salem (the city that would become Jerusalem)—brought out bread and wine (Genesis 14:18). The author of Genesis writes that this king *was priest of God Most High, and he blessed Abram, saying, "Blessed be Abram by God Most High, Creator of heaven and earth. And praise be to God Most High, who delivered your enemies into your hand"* (verses 18–20). At this point, the Bible records that Abram gave the king *a tenth of everything* (verse 20).

It's important to see the timing here. Abram doesn't give a tithe to the priest in order to gain a blessing or God's favor. He'd already won the battle. He had his nephew and everyone's possessions back from those who had taken it all. Instead, Abram offered the tithe in acknowledgement of God's blessing and favor.

The second mention of a tithe in the Bible comes many years later with Jacob, one of Abram's grandsons, and it can easily be misconstrued if you don't know the whole story. Jacob is on a journey to his mother's relatives so he can choose a wife. One night, he lies down to sleep and experiences something incredible.

> *He had a dream in which he saw a stairway resting on the earth, with its top reaching to heaven, and the angels of God were ascending and descending on it. There above it stood the Lord, and He said: "I am the Lord, the God of your father Abraham and the God of Isaac. I will give you and your descendants the land on which you are lying"* (Genesis 28:12–13).

When Jacob wakes up the next morning, he makes a vow. *If God will be with me and will watch over me on this journey I am taking and will give me food to eat and clothes to wear so that I return safely to my father's household, then the Lord will be my God and this stone that I have set up as a pillar will be God's house, and of all that you give me I will give you a tenth* (verses 20–22).

If you only knew this much, it would seem like Jacob was buying God's favor. It appears as if Jacob is striking a deal something along the lines of, "If you take care of me, I'll pay you homage." But Jacob's story mirrors Abram's more closely than you may think. In the dream, the Lord actually promises Jacob six things:

1. *I will give you and your descendants the land on which you are lying* (verse 13).
2. *Your descendants will be like the dust of the earth, and you will spread out to the west and to the east, to the north and to the south* (verse 14).
3. *All peoples on earth will be blessed through you and your offspring* (verse 14).
4. *I am with you and will watch over you wherever you go* (verse 15).
5. *I will bring you back to this land* (verse 15).
6. *I will not leave you until I have done what I have promised you* (verse 15).

So Jacob's vow, just like Abram's offering, was a response to God's blessing and favor.

The True Purpose of the Tithe

The law recorded in Leviticus, Numbers, and Deuteronomy includes many instructions for tithing. The Israelites were reminded that the tithe *belongs to the Lord; it is holy to the Lord* (Leviticus 27:30). Even the Levites (the tribe of Israel responsible for the religious activities of the nation) who received their wages and support from the tithe were to give ten percent from what they received (Numbers 18:25–26). In returning this portion to God, all the Jews mentally, emotionally, and symbolically recognized God's provision for today and their dependence upon Him for tomorrow.

In addition to supporting the priests (Levites) and the Tabernacle, the tithe was used to support community festivals, orphans, widows, and travelers (Deuteronomy 12:5–7; 14:22–23, 27–29). God was serious about His people understanding that the tithe was a big deal. Malachi 3:8–12 says,

> *"Will a mere mortal rob God? Yet you rob Me.*
>
> *"But you ask, 'How are we robbing You?'*
>
> *"In tithes and offerings. You are under a curse—your whole nation—because you are robbing Me. Bring the whole tithe into the storehouse, that there may be food in My house. Test Me in this," says the Lord Almighty, "and see if I will not throw open the floodgates of heaven and pour out so much blessing that there will not be room enough to store it. I will prevent pests from devouring your crops, and the vines in your fields will not drop their fruit before it is ripe," says the Lord Almighty. "Then all the nations will call you blessed, for yours will be a delightful land," says the Lord Almighty.*

This is where tithing gets murky for some. By including the provision in the law and by stating that not paying it is robbing God, people equate tithing to an obligation. And while it is something God expects of us, reducing the tithe to merely a debt or requirement makes it easy to take out the heart of its practice.

Tithing is about understanding that God is sovereign. He has supreme power and authority, which means He owns everything and can do with it what He chooses (Psalm 24:1, 115:3). In His wisdom, He elects to allow us a portion to use as we see fit. By giving back to Him a small percentage, we acknowledge His rule and show appreciation for all He's given us. It's a response of love—just like it was for both Abram and Jacob.

Questions About the Tithe

Once we know that tithing is a response of love and an acknowledgement of God's sovereignty, we can understand that it isn't a salvation issue. God isn't sitting in heaven waiting for you to mess this up so He can zap you with a heavenly lightning bolt.

However, we need to prayerfully consider some of the common controversies around the tithe:

- Do we tithe off our gross or net income?
- Do we tithe on cash we receive for birthdays and other holidays?
- Does all the tithe go to a local church? Or can some be given to other local (or national, or global) charities?
- What's the difference between tithes and offerings?
- What if I can't tithe money? Can I give something else, like my time?

You may not like this, but I'm not going to give you a lot of hard and fast answers here. Some of these questions are between you and God, and only He has the answer that's right for you. Here's what I can offer.

First, some believe your tithe should go to your local church. In the verses from Malachi that I quoted above, the Lord says, *Bring the whole tithe into the storehouse, that there may be food in my house* (Malachi 3:10). The *storehouse* the verse refers to was the Temple in Jerusalem, the place the Jews went to worship. Some interpret that to mean in today's world the local church while others argue that it should be a denominational or national lead organization. My advice is to ask God where He wants you to give your tithe and follow His instructions.

However you choose, do not ignore Paul's advice in 2 Corinthians 9:7. He writes, *Each of you should give what you have decided in your heart to give, not reluctantly or under compulsion, for God loves a cheerful giver.* Cheerful tithing includes trusting the church or charity's leadership to faithfully steward what God provides. No organization will do this perfectly, but if you question whether the leaders are honoring God with the church or company's finances, don't withhold your tithe; prayerfully consider finding a new church or charity.

Once you give ten percent of your financial income to your church or other organization, additional donations are an offering. Dozens of excellent ministries exist around the world, and God gave us each unique hearts leaning toward different causes so that all would benefit. And you can bless these organizations with much more than just your money; you can offer your time, talents, and possessions. Your strengths, gifts, and training isn't for your benefit alone, but should be used *to serve others, as faithful stewards of God's grace in its various forms* (1 Peter 4:10).

No matter your talent or training, it can be easy to discount the value of what comes easily for you, but we should fight against that tendency. Paul writes in Romans 12:6–8, *We have different gifts, according to the grace given to each of us. If your gift is prophesying, then prophesy in accordance with your faith; if it is serving, then serve; if it is teaching, then teach; if it is to encourage, then give encouragement; if it is giving, then give generously; if it is to lead, do it diligently; if it is to show mercy, do it cheerfully.* And the writer of Hebrews reminds us that God is paying attention. *God is not unjust; He will not forget your work and the love you have shown Him as you have helped His people and continue to help them* (Hebrews 6:10).

Outside of those guidelines, pray. Read your Bible and ask God for clarity on what He wants you to do with your tithes and offerings.

Think About It

1. What do you think about tithing? How much do you mindlessly consume God's blessings and provisions?

2. Mark 12:41–44 tells the story of a poor widow who gave everything she had. Take stock of your life and your finances. How much do you trust God to provide for tomorrow? Where do things need to change to better align with God's heart on tithing?

3. Second Corinthians 9:7 says, *Each of you should give what you have decided in your heart to give, not reluctantly or under compulsion, for God loves a cheerful giver.* Where do you most struggle in tithing: Giving money to God, feeling like you *have* to give, or trusting Him to provide for tomorrow? Talk to God about this, and ask Him to help you.

Chapter Six: Fellowship

A Summary

The Greek words usually translated *fellowship* in the New Testament are koinoinia (noun) or koinonein (verb), and they were routinely used in four different situations: In a business partnership, in a marriage or family relationship, in relation to a god, and to refer to the spirit of generosity. The different usages can be seen in different places in the Bible. For example, Luke 5:10 talks about business partners James and John (koinonos), and Hebrews 2:14 calls on the family usage when it says we are people of flesh and blood (koinonein).

To get to the level of what God desires, though—that third usage of the word—we need to start with the apostles John and Paul.

Consider 1 John 1:3–7.

We proclaim to you what we have seen and heard, so that you also may have fellowship with us. And our fellowship is with the Father and with His Son, Jesus Christ. We write this to make our joy complete.

This is the message we have heard from Him and declare to you: God is light; in Him there is no darkness at all. If we claim to have fellowship with Him and yet walk in the darkness, we lie and do not live out the truth. But if we walk in the light, as He is in the light, we have fellowship with one another, and the blood of Jesus, His Son, purifies us from all sin.

Consider Romans 12:4–5.
For just as each of us has one body with many members, and these members do not all have the same function, so in Christ we, though many, form one body, and each member belongs to all the others.

What Else Does Fellowship Look Like?

Consider Proverbs 27:17
As iron sharpens iron, so one person sharpens another.

Consider Colossians 3:16
Let the message of Christ dwell among you richly as you teach and admonish one another with all wisdom through psalms, hymns, and songs from the Spirit, singing to God with gratitude in your hearts.

Consider Hebrews 10:24–25
We should keep on encouraging each other to be thoughtful and to do helpful things. Some people have gotten out of the habit of meeting for worship, but we must not do that. We should keep on encouraging each other, especially since you know that the day of the Lord's coming is getting closer.

Fellowship

More Detail

Are you a people person or not? God made both, so both are good! But, this chapter might be a little easier for those who love and are energized by people.

In a broad sense, I am an introvert. It's not that I don't like people; it's just that being around them exhausts me. Being social does not come naturally to me, so I use up a lot of energy in groups even when it appears that I am doing nothing but listening to the conversation. When I go on vacation, I can happily dis-regard everyone I don't know. While my kids are splashing around a pool, I'm content sitting quietly in a hot tub with no bubbles. I value stillness. I need a measure of silence in my daily life.

Most people don't have a problem with at least some social interaction. Even in my quiet nature, I recognize that I also need a portion of time with others. But is fellowship at church really necessary? Maybe you've been hurt by people—maybe Christians in a church. Perhaps you like people, but sitting still through an hour-long service is your issue. How does attending church count as spending time with people anyway when the interaction with them is so limited? I think a large part of the problem with fellowship is that we don't really understand what it is.

Let's start by defining *fellowship*. Among the seven definitions, dictionary.com includes:

- friendly relationship; companionship
- community of interest, feeling, etc.

- an association of persons having similar tastes, interests, etc.[1]

Churches use the word in various ways, adding to the confusion. Sometimes they mean an informal gathering where food is served. Other times they mean the communication that naturally happens when people get together. None of that is very helpful in figuring out what God expects from us when it comes to biblical fellowship.

Acts 2 records four specific things the early church did that produced amazing results.

They devoted themselves to the apostles' teaching and to fellowship, to the breaking of bread and to prayer. Everyone was filled with awe at the many wonders and signs performed by the apostles. All the believers were together and had everything in common. They sold property and possessions to give to anyone who had need. Every day they continued to meet together in the temple courts. They broke bread in their homes and ate together with glad and sincere hearts, praising God and enjoying the favor of all the people. And the Lord added to their number daily those who were being saved (Acts 2:42–47).

Just think about it! The leaders did miracles, the believers experienced unity, and everyone helped fulfill the needs of others. They met daily, ate together, praised God, and enjoyed the favor of others. All because the Christians devoted themselves to teaching, to fellowship, to the breaking of bread, and to prayer. If we want what the early church had, we should start by figuring out what they did.

Consider the Greek

The Greek words usually translated *fellowship* in the New Testament are koinoinia (noun) or koinonein (verb), and they were routinely used in four different situations: In a business partnership, in a marriage or family relationship, in relation to a god, and to refer to the spirit of generosity. The different usages can be seen in different places in the Bible. For example, Luke 5:10 talks about business partners James and John (koinonos), and Hebrews 2:14 calls on the family usage when it says we are people of flesh and blood (koinonein).

To get to the level of what God desires, though—that third usage of the word—we need to look to the apostles John and Paul. Look first at 1 John 1:3–7.

> *We proclaim to you what we have seen and heard, so that you also may have fellowship with us. And our fellowship is with the Father and with His Son, Jesus Christ. We write this to make our joy complete.*

> *This is the message we have heard from Him and declare to you: God is light; in Him there is no darkness at all. If we claim to have fellowship with Him and yet walk in the darkness, we lie and do not live out the truth. But if we walk in the light, as He is in the light, we have fellowship with one another, and the blood of Jesus, His Son, purifies us from all sin.*

I know we're going a little deep here, but stick with me! In the verses above, John draws upon the usage of the word we're looking for, a relationship with God. But he pushes us to think bigger. I love how the Contemporary English Version translates verse 7. *If we live in the light, as God does, we share in life with each other*!

Paul agrees with John and expands on this concept in several places. In 1 Corinthians 1:9 he writes that God has called us *into fellowship with His Son, Jesus*. We've already talked about the symbolism of baptism in chapter 2, and Paul pulls on that while reinforcing the connection we have with Christ in Romans 6:4. *We were therefore buried with Him through baptism into death in order that, just as Christ was raised from the dead through the glory of the Father, we too may live a new life.*

Perhaps the passage that gives us a clear example of what Paul is trying to convey is Romans 12:4–5. He writes, *For just as each of us has one body with many members, and these members do not all have the same function, so in Christ we, though many, form one body, and each member belongs to all the others*. In other words, each of us has a heart, lungs, a liver, skin, and hundreds of other pieces, each focused on its own function; yet it is one body. The moment we accept Christ, we join with Him and thousands of other believers. Just like the parts of our body, we each have our own function (passions, talents, gifts, jobs, assignments), but also just like our body, we are one—in Christ. When we think of fellowship with other Christians, we must consider it in this deeper concept.

The practical reality of this quickly becomes apparent with a little thought. Again, consider your body. We know that cardio exercise benefits the heart and lungs. But anything that profits one part of our body is an asset to every other part of our body. What good is the foot if the heart is too weak to allow us to walk across the room?

It is in this logical extension of spiritual fellowship that Paul writes commands such as *Carry each other's burdens, and in this way you will fulfill the law of Christ* (Galatians 6:2). And, *share with the Lord's people who are in need. Practice hospitality* (Romans 12:13).

This type of fellowship values our Christian brothers and

sisters and their contributions to the church, the community, and the world. It takes seriously Paul's statement that each of us is *filled with knowledge and competent to instruct one another* (Romans 15:14), and believes *that if two of you on earth agree about anything they ask for, it will be done for them* (Matthew 18:19).

What Else Does Fellowship Look Like?

Besides what we've already talked about (sharing with others, hospitality, teaching), what else does this look like? The potluck meal at church falls under sharing and hospitality, and Sunday school could be teaching, but is that all we need to worry about?

Remember that God is always after our heart—the motives behind what we do. So it's more important that we have a heart to give and to serve than that we spend hours listening to teachers or making food for others. That doesn't get you out of fellowship! It's just a reminder to check your heart and ask God how you are doing.

Here are some verses to consider as you think about fellowship, how God designed you, and where God wants you to join with other Christians.

***I rejoiced with those who said to me, "Let us go to the house of the Lord"* (Psalm 122:1).**

For those who are in Christ (i.e., saved, have Jesus in their heart and life), going to church is just meeting up with other parts of the body of Christ. Lots can happen within the church to increase fellowship, from praise to prayer to teaching to eating together. Never discount what God can do in your life when you make regular church attendance a priority.

As iron sharpens iron, so one person sharpens another **(Proverbs 27:17).**

Being around people does many things. In large groups and small groups, other people might reveal problems in your heart or your thinking. They may provide just the encouragement you need to recover after a tough week or the motivation to tackle the obstacle in front of you. But others do this best when you take the time to form relationships. Get involved with a ministry and join a small group. When you find a good group that fits you well, the benefits to your heart and life far outweigh the difficulty in finding them.

So Christ Himself gave the apostles, the prophets, the evangelists, the pastors and teachers, to equip His people for works of service, so that the body of Christ may be built up until we all reach unity in the faith and in the knowledge of the Son of God and become mature, attaining to the whole measure of the fullness of Christ **(Ephesians 4:11–13).**

God didn't assign people to stand over us preaching just to test our ability to sit still and stay awake. Evangelists, pastors, and other teachers are charged with equipping us to serve. It is our job to serve so that other Christians will be built up. And this all works together so that *we will grow to become in every respect the mature body of Him who is the head, that is, Christ. From Him the whole body, joined and held together by every supporting ligament, grows and builds itself up in love, as each part does its work* (verses 15–16).

What does that mean in plain language? Regular people like you and me join together as we search to know God and understand the Bible, caring for each other's needs and working together to fulfill everything Christ wants to accomplish on this earth. Isn't that a beautiful, hope-filled picture?

But it only happens when we join together. Sitting at home watching church on your laptop isn't going to cut it. Neither is walking into a church before a service and walking out again immediately afterward without taking the time to talk to others.

Let the message of Christ dwell among you richly as you teach and admonish one another with all wisdom through psalms, hymns, and songs from the Spirit, singing to God with gratitude in your hearts **(Colossians 3:16).**

The music lovers among us will be happy. Yes, the Bible says we should teach through psalms (another word for songs), hymns, and songs. Just don't miss the phrase *with all wisdom*. That means you need to be reading your Bible and asking God for understanding so you have some wisdom to share through your music.

We should keep on encouraging each other to be thoughtful and to do helpful things. Some people have gotten out of the habit of meeting for worship, but we must not do that. We should keep on encouraging each other, especially since you know that the day of the Lord's coming is getting closer **(Hebrews 10:24–25).**

The writer of Hebrews was an encourager. But we need to realize how difficult it is to encourage someone else if you have no idea what is going on in his life. And the best way to be involved on this level is to participate in small groups and small Sunday school classes.

The author also makes it pretty clear that gathering together with others for the express purpose of worship is something we must do.

Think About It

1. Does the thought of regular fellowship excite you? Why or why not?

2. Are you more drawn to large group fellowship (church services, church-wide dinners) or small group fellowship (Bible studies, having dinner with one or two other families)? Why is that the better or easier choice for you?

3. What bothers you most about the other choice from question 2 (large or small group fellowship)? What can you do to make it better or easier for you to participate in?

---

[7] "Fellowship." *Dictionary.com*. Dictionary.com, n.d. Web. 25 Apr. 2017.

Part Three
Final Thoughts

Chapter Seven: Wrapping It Up

You Did It!

You made it all the way to the end of this book. I'm so proud of you. I've thrown a lot of information and Bible verses at you, and some of it will take you some time to process. That's okay! You'll soon realize that you have a lot more to learn about almost everything we've discussed in these pages.

God will never let you down, and as you following the four principles of growth—Bible reading, prayer, tithing, and fellowship—He will guide you to change in ways that you can't presently imagine. One step of obedience at a time, one day at a time, you will gradually become more knowledgeable about God, more trusting of Christ, and more dependent on the Holy Spirit.

As you take your next steps on this amazing journey, I pray for you what the apostle Paul prayed for one of the churches he started.

> *When I think of all this, I fall to my knees and pray to the Father, the Creator of everything in heaven and on earth. I pray that from his glorious, unlimited resources he will empower you with inner strength through his Spirit. Then Christ will make his home in your hearts as you trust in him. Your roots will grow down into God's love and keep you strong. And may you have the power to understand, as all God's people should, how wide, how long, how high, and how deep his love is. May you experience the love of Christ, though it is too great to understand fully. Then you will be made complete with all the fullness of life and power that comes from God.*

Now all glory to God, who is able, through his mighty power at work within us, to accomplish infinitely more than we might ask or think. Glory to him in the church and in Christ Jesus through all generations forever and ever! Amen (Ephesians 3:14–21, New Living Translation).

Appendix

Recommended Resources

These resources are listed in alphabetical order by book title. This list is not all-inclusive but includes items I found helpful.

Recommended Books and Websites

Any books by E.M. Bounds on prayer, to include *The Complete Works of E.M. Bounds: Power Through Prayer; Prayer and Praying Men; The Essentials of Prayer; The Necessity of Prayer; The Possibilities of Prayer; Purpose in Prayer; The Weapon of Prayer*

The Case for a Creator: A Journalist Investigates Scientific Evidence That Points Toward God, The Case for Christ: A Journalist's Personal Investigation of the Evidence for Jesus, and *The Case for Faith: A Journalist Investigates the Toughest Objections to Christianity* by Lee Strobel. Also, www.leestrobel.com – Lee Strobel's website. Includes a newsletter, videos, and a schedule of where he's speaking.

Discerning the Voice of God: How to Recognize When He Speaks by Priscilla Shirer

Essential Truths of the Christian Faith by R.C. Sproul. Also, www.ligonier.org – R.C. Sproul's website. Includes broadcasts, devotions, books and links to free eBook downloads.

The Power of a Praying Husband by Michael and Stormie Omartian. Also, *The Power of a Praying Wife* by Stormie Omartian

Praying God's Will for My Daughter and *Praying God's Will for My Son* by Lee Roberts

The Total Money Makeover: A Proven Plan for Financial Fitness by Dave Ramsey

Why I Believe by D. James Kennedy

Also by Carrie Daws
Crossing Series

Book 1: *Crossing Values*: For years, Amber traipsed around the Northwest avoiding the skeletons in her closet. As winter plants itself firmly across the Rockies, she decides to take a chance on a job at a logging company with a family different from any she's ever known before. Could they truly be genuine? Could Faye understand the trauma from her past or Peter think of her as more than just the winter office help? Could this family really hold the key to what she's seeking?

Book 2, *Ryan's Crossing*: After ten years, Ryan's parents found his runaway sister. As he meets her before her wedding, he must decide where she will fit into his life and what his future will look like. Seeing the town where his sister lives only brings more questions. Portland may be the better choice for him in his upcoming move, but small town life appeals to him. Is it the friendly people or the sister of the groom?

Book 3, *Romancing Melody*: A Crossing Journey: Newlywed Melody Podell gives up everything she has ever known to follow her husband, a soldier in the US Army, to Fort Bragg, NC. Soon after giving birth to their first child and dealing with her husband's deployment to a dangerous part of the world, tragedy strikes forcing Melody to travel back to home. Walking back into the lives of her old friends in Crossing, Oregon, is the last thing Melody wants to do, but could she be missing something? Is God really in control?

Book 4, *Crossing's Redemption*: Many would describe Patricia Guire as an eclectic force to be reckoned with, but something is wrong. Amber Yager feels called to love on her, yet as she discovers Patricia's hidden past, she is drawn in to a group that brings disquiet to her own soul. Will the love she's found in Crossing be taken from her? Or could Amber and Patricia find peace as God shines light into the darkest places of their hearts?

Embers Series

Book 1, *Kindling Embers*: Inspector Cassandra McCarthy never thought she'd be raising her two daughters alone, but her husband's unexpected death forced her to find a career. Now working beside a retired Special Operations soldier and veteran fireman, she serves her small North Carolina town, protecting them from hazards they don't understand. She loves what she does and trusts God to provide—until a series of unexplained fires hits too close to home.

Book 2, *Igniting Embers*: Deputy Fire Marshal Cassandra McCarthy thought her life would settle down once the teenagers who had been starting nuisance fires were caught. But a hurricane heading to Silver Heights threatens to destroy both property and lives, and another unexplained fire evokes fears of a serial arsonist. Can she prepare the town for the looming emergency and protect them from the danger living in their midst?

Book 3, *Extinguishing Embers*: The hurricane left millions of dollars of destruction, and the Federal Emergency Management Agency has invaded to help the community clean up and move forward. Yet in the midst of recovery, a rash of unexplained fires grow more menacing. Deputy Fire Marshal Cassandra

McCarthy works closely with the sheriff's office and the county fire departments, following the small pieces of evidence left at each fire scene. But what will it cost her to capture the arsonist?

The Warrior's Bride: Biblical Strategies to Help the Military Spouse Thrive

The call came down from Command, and your warrior husband is out the door, leaving you behind to handle whatever he has left undone. Whether it's the day-to-day monotony, the inevitable appliance that breaks, or the months without his presence beside you, being a military spouse brings challenges few appreciate. Yet God see you and longs for you to boldly step into His plan. He purposely chose you for this moment—for your man. He wants to give you abundantly more than what you have right now and desires you to thrive as your warrior's bride.

"Wow! This book is fantastic. It's a wonderful treasure of information for married women . . . military and civilian. Even though the authors promote this book as advice for military spouses, all of the principles and guidance found here are applicable for any married woman . . . If I could give this book six stars, I would. But I give it five stars, and firmly believe, it's worth every star!"
~Author Joanie Bruce, *Alana Candler, Marked for Murder*

Beyond The Warrior's Bride Series

Book 1: Your Extended Family: A Military Spouse's Biblical Guide to Surviving Within and Without Your Family

Family. They can be one of our biggest blessings and one of our biggest stressors. Family members that don't understand the military system can complicate your life, and sometimes the best-intentioned relative can undercut everything you are trying to build with your husband. Living far away can also be hard if you have a medical emergency. Deployments and high ops tempos give loneliness and depression the opportunity to take over. Are there really any practical answers? What does the Bible say about dealing with and living apart from family?

Book 2: Reintegration: A Military Spouse's Biblical Guide to Surviving after the Homecoming

Deployments are inevitable in military life. Short or long, relatively safe or extremely dangerous, time away from our men is standard issue. How can the family left behind best deal with the transition before and after deployment? And what should we do if he comes home different? Those who deal with long separations due to a career know that the first weeks back can be trickier than when you first began living together as a couple, particularly if the mission was stressful or life-threatening. While the Bible doesn't specifically mention reintegration, God still gives us great advice on preparing our hearts and minds so that our marriage can thrive even through Reintegration.

Book 3: Moving: A Military Spouse's Biblical Guide to Surviving a PCS

We've got orders! As many military spouses know, these simple words change your life. Whether you are moving just a couple of states over or around the world, a flurry of activity is about to consume your calendar. Where do you start? How do you begin to process all your emotions or prepare your children to say goodbye to their friends? How do you know if you need to host a yard sale or even what your weight limit is? Take a deep breath and know that help is available. This book and the free moving checklist will get you started in the right direction.

Book 4: Finances: A Military Spouse's Biblical Guide to Personal Finance

Money. It's one of the biggest stressors in marriages. Many live paycheck-to-paycheck, struggling to both cover all the bills and save for retirement. Often husband and wife disagree over petty expenses, forgetting that they are on the same team. But money doesn't have to be a constant battle. Not only does the Bible give a lot of guidance, but God also provided examples of people getting it right. With a shift in focus and a little disciplined effort, you can gain control over your finances instead of your finances controlling you.

Book 5: Other Military Spouses: A Military Spouse's Biblical Guide to Finding Great Friends

Other military spouses can be one of the biggest stressors in a wife's life. From gossipers to spouse shamers, the problem is reaching epidemic proportions, and many don't know what to do about it. What if you could find a better way? Instead of attacking the problem-women head on or avoiding all women entirely, what if you could find women worth knowing and cherishing? No matter where you are, God placed around you women of great value, women who strive to love Him first, and women who want to love and encourage you. Instead of resigning your-self to a life of loneliness, let me show you who to avoid and what characteristics to look for in quality friends.

Book 6: Retirement: A Military Spouse's Biblical Guide to Life beyond the Military

The years have been hard, filled with deployments, trainings, moves, forced flexibility, and uncertainty. Retirement finally looms, yet a fresh uncertainty takes hold. Gone are the days of someone telling you where to live and providing a house for you. No longer will someone tell your man where to go and what to take with him. Now all those choices are yours and his. Where do you start? Among the plethora of options open to you, pieces of the military will likely always follow you. As your ETS (Expiration Term of Service) nears, learn from retired military spouses Kathy Barnett and Carrie Daws, who have already walked the road you face. Make the journey forward a little easier by arming yourself with what they've discovered in retirement.

COMING SOON:
A NEW HOME FOR ALLIE

Allie loves her home in Kenya. But her dad works for the Animal Jungle Patrol, and he just got orders to move their family to Somalia. She has many questions, and the journey will be long. Will the new place be like what she knows? Will she find friends in her new home? And will she ever see her best friend again?

For more information about
Carrie Daws
please visit:

www.CarrieDaws.com
Contact@CarrieDaws.com
Facebook.com/CarrieDaws
@CarrieDaws

Made in the USA
San Bernardino, CA
03 December 2018